MY BEST BOOK OF
WHALES
AND DOLPHINS

Christiane Gunzi

KINGFISHER
LONDON & NEW YORK

KINGFISHER
LONDON & NEW YORK

Copyright © Macmillan Children's Books 2001, 2006, 2019
First published 2001 in the United States by Kingfisher
This edition published 2019 by Kingfisher
120 Broadway, New York, NY 10271
Kingfisher is an imprint of Macmillan Children's Books, London
All rights reserved.

Distributed in the U.S. and Canada by Macmillan,
120 Broadway, New York, NY 10271

Library of Congress Cataloging-in-Publication data has
been applied for.

ISBN 978-0-7534-7525-6

Design by Wildpixel Ltd.
Illustrations: Michael Langham Rowe, William Oliver,
  Jim Channell
Consultants: Julie Childs and Theresa Greenaway

Kingfisher books are available for special promotions and
premiums. For details contact: Special Markets Department,
Macmillan, 120 Broadway, New York, NY 10271

For more information please visit:
www.kingfisherbooks.com

Printed in China
10 9 8 7 6 5 4 3 2 1
1TR/0719/UG/WKT/128MA

The Publisher would like to thank the following for permission to
reproduce their material.
Top = t; Bottom = b; Center = c; Left = l; Right = r
Front cover Yann-HUBERT/iStock, skynesher/iStock; Back cover
Baptiste/iStock; 2-3 facanv/Shutterstock; 4-5 malija/iStock;
6-7 zynatis/Shutterstock; 8-9, 32 Mumemories/iStock;10-11 bg zynatis/
Shutterstock; 12-13 zynatis/Shutterstock; 14-15 William Bradberry/
Shutterstock; 18 John Gaffen 2/Alamy Stock Photos; 18-19 John
Tunnery/Shutterstock; 20 Design Pics Inc/Alamy Stock Photos;
21 William Bradberry/Shutterstock; 22 Sunwand24/Shutterstock;
22-23 Wild_and_free_naturephoto/Shutterstock; 23 Elise Lefran/
Shutterstock; 24-25 Benny Marty/Shutterstock; 26-27 Neil Bradfield/
Shutterstock; 28-29 Torontonian/Alamy Stock Photos; 29 Gonzalo
Jara/Shutterstock; 30 Kevin Schafer/Alamy Stock Photos, Kit Korzun/
Shutterstock; 31 Roka/Shutterstock

CONTENTS

MEET THE WHALES

Whales are the largest sea creatures on Earth, and the blue whale is the biggest animal ever known. Whales are divided into two groups. Toothed whales include dolphins and porpoises, and baleen whales include blue whales and humpback whales. Whales are mammals, and they are found in every ocean. Some have lived for up to 200 years!

Dolphin or porpoise?

Porpoises and dolphins are much smaller than whales. A dolphin has a slim body with pointed fins. It also has a beak. A porpoise has no beak, and it is plumper than a dolphin. Its fins are short and more blunt. One kind of porpoise has no fins at all.

Hourglass dolphin

Dall's porpoise

Gentle giants

Blue whales spend the summers in the Arctic and Antarctic oceans, where there is plenty of krill and plankton to eat. In the winter, these whales travel to warm waters to breed. Females give birth to one baby every two or three years. A newborn calf usually weighs over three tons!

ADULT BLUE WHALE

An adult blue whale measures up to 85 feet (26 meters) in length, and can weigh up to 100 tons

BLUE WHALE CALF

A blue whale calf drinks 158 gallons (600 liters) of its mother's milk every day for seven months before it begins to eat other food

THE FIRST WHALES

About 55 million years ago, some of the mammals that lived on land moved to live in the sea. They may have been looking for food there. Over millions of years, these mammals gradually adapted to living underwater, and slowly evolved into the first kinds of whales. Two of the earliest whales were *Basilosaurus* and *Durodon*. *Basilosaurus* was as big as a sperm whale!

Sea monster

Basilosaurus lived between 38 and 45 million years ago, and *Durodon* lived 25 million years ago. *Basilosaurus* was about 75 feet (23 meters) long and weighed at least five tons. This carnivore hunted other sea creatures.

Basilosaurus had big teeth for catching other sea creatures

Old and new

The teeth of the first whales, such as *Basilosaurus*, were a mixture of sizes and shapes. But a modern whale, such as the killer whale, has teeth that are all alike. Ancient whales had nostrils near the front of the head, but whales today have nostrils much farther back. These nostrils are the whale's blowhole.

Nostril

Killer whale skull

Nostril

Basilosaurus skull

A WORLD OF WHALES

There are about 11 different kinds of baleen whale and 67 kinds of toothed whale, including dolphins and porpoises. Some whales, such as the blue whale and humpback, are enormous—others are very small. The color of a whale helps it blend in with its surroundings. Most whales are blue-gray, to match the sea. Belugas are white, and narwhals are mottled black and white. This helps camouflage them in their icy Arctic home.

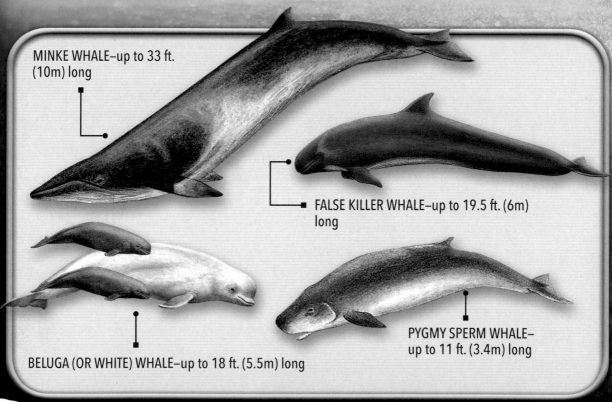

MINKE WHALE–up to 33 ft. (10m) long

FALSE KILLER WHALE–up to 19.5 ft. (6m) long

PYGMY SPERM WHALE–up to 11 ft. (3.4m) long

BELUGA (OR WHITE) WHALE–up to 18 ft. (5.5m) long

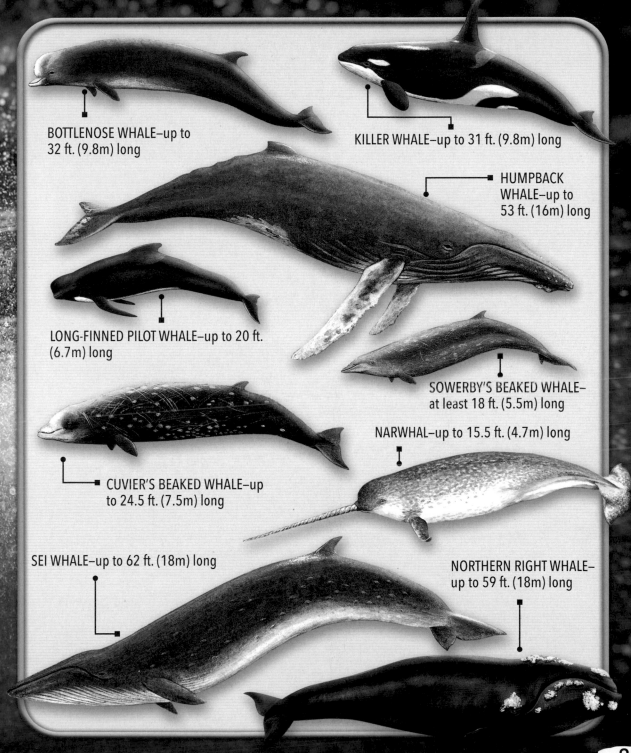

BOTTLENOSE WHALE–up to 32 ft. (9.8m) long

KILLER WHALE–up to 31 ft. (9.8m) long

HUMPBACK WHALE–up to 53 ft. (16m) long

LONG-FINNED PILOT WHALE–up to 20 ft. (6.7m) long

SOWERBY'S BEAKED WHALE–at least 18 ft. (5.5m) long

NARWHAL–up to 15.5 ft. (4.7m) long

CUVIER'S BEAKED WHALE–up to 24.5 ft. (7.5m) long

SEI WHALE–up to 62 ft. (18m) long

NORTHERN RIGHT WHALE–up to 59 ft. (18m) long

A WORLD OF DOLPHINS

There are more than 30 kinds of dolphins and six kinds of porpoises. Most dolphins live in the ocean. Some dolphins live in rivers, so they are known as freshwater or river dolphins. Porpoises usually live in small groups near the coast. Dolphins and porpoises are closely related, but they belong to separate families and are different in shape.

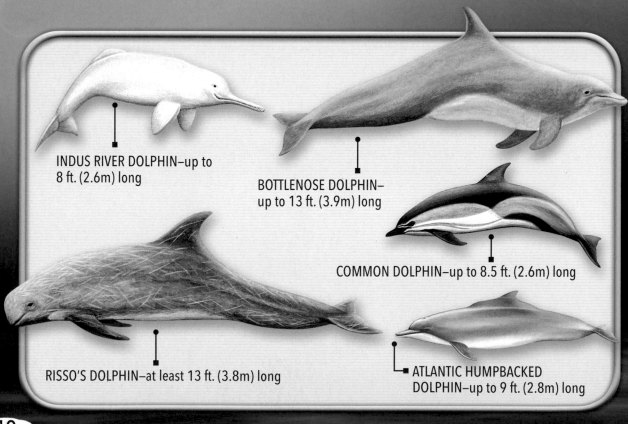

INDUS RIVER DOLPHIN–up to 8 ft. (2.6m) long

BOTTLENOSE DOLPHIN– up to 13 ft. (3.9m) long

COMMON DOLPHIN–up to 8.5 ft. (2.6m) long

RISSO'S DOLPHIN–at least 13 ft. (3.8m) long

ATLANTIC HUMPBACKED DOLPHIN–up to 9 ft. (2.8m) long

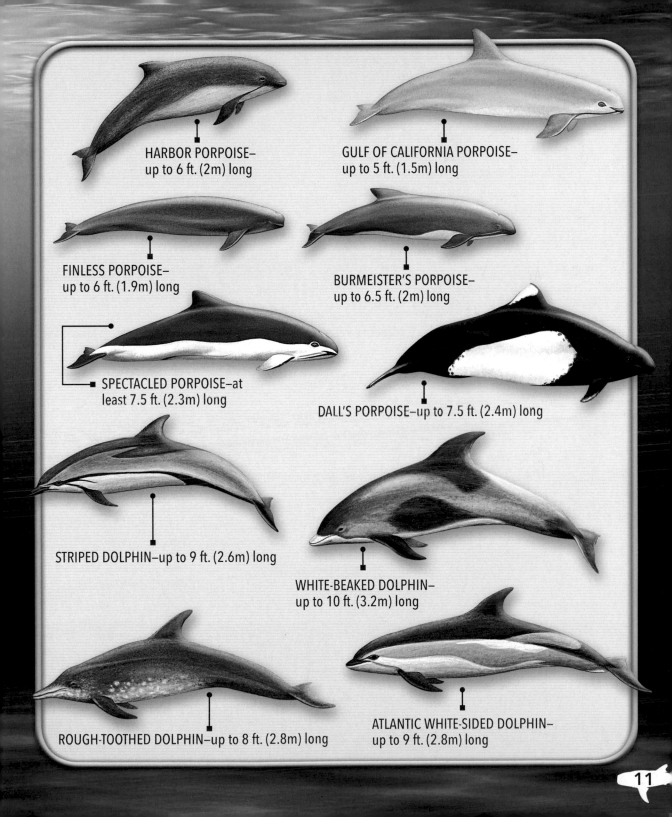

HARBOR PORPOISE–
up to 6 ft. (2m) long

GULF OF CALIFORNIA PORPOISE–
up to 5 ft. (1.5m) long

FINLESS PORPOISE–
up to 6 ft. (1.9m) long

BURMEISTER'S PORPOISE–
up to 6.5 ft. (2m) long

SPECTACLED PORPOISE–at
least 7.5 ft. (2.3m) long

DALL'S PORPOISE–up to 7.5 ft. (2.4m) long

STRIPED DOLPHIN–up to 9 ft. (2.6m) long

WHITE-BEAKED DOLPHIN–
up to 10 ft. (3.2m) long

ROUGH-TOOTHED DOLPHIN–up to 8 ft. (2.8m) long

ATLANTIC WHITE-SIDED DOLPHIN–
up to 9 ft. (2.8m) long

LIFE IN THE OCEANS

Most whales, dolphins, and porpoises live in the open ocean, and they are superb swimmers. Some of the largest animals spend some of their time alone, but whales, dolphins, and porpoises usually live in groups. Large groups are called herds, and there can be thousands of dolphins in a single herd. All whales are very acrobatic and often leap right out of the water.

Breaching whale
When whales rise up out of the water then fall onto their backs with a huge splash, it is called breaching. Nobody is sure why whales breach. Perhaps they do it just for fun!

Barnacles, lice, and worms live on this whale's head in lumps called bonnets

Leaping dolphins

Dolphins are playful creatures. They enjoy racing through the water and jumping high into the air. When they leap out of the water in a curve, it's called porpoising. Dolphins do this more often than porpoises!

Southern right whale dolphins porpoising

BLOWHOLES

A whale or dolphin breathes through a blowhole on top of its head. A baleen whale has two blowholes, and a toothed whale has one. The blowhole can open when the whale swims to the surface for air and then close again when it goes back underwater. Some sperm whales can hold their breath underwater for two hours or more.

Spout shapes

The spout coming out of the blowhole is the whale's warm breath, which contains water vapor. Vapor is a mist that is made when the whale's breath mixes with cold air. Scientists recognize whales by the shape of their spouts.

Spout is large and spread out

FIN WHALES

Spout is low

BOWHEAD WHALES

SPERM WHALES

Spout points to the left

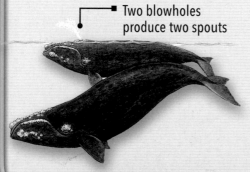

Two blowholes produce two spouts

NORTHERN RIGHT WHALES

Deepest diver

The sperm whale is the largest toothed whale. It can measure up to 65 feet (20 meters) long. Sperm whales can dive deeper than any other sea mammal, reaching depths of 10,000 feet (3,000 meters) or more. When a sperm whale swims to the surface to blow air out of its blowhole, there is a large cloud of vapor and a thunderous sound like an explosion!

A sperm whale flicks its tail as it dives down to catch fish and squid on the seabed

HUNTING FOR PREY

The killer whale, or orca, is the only whale that hunts other sea mammals. It has sharp, cone-shaped teeth for grabbing prey. Killer whales eat seals and dolphins and sometimes attack other whales. Dolphins, porpoises, sperm whales, and pilot whales are also toothed whales. They hunt fish and squid and usually swallow their food whole.

Teamwork

Killer whales work in teams to catch their prey, and then they share their meal. They usually hunt for seals swimming near the seashore. Sometimes a killer whale will almost swim onto the beach to grab a seal.

What toothed whales eat

Most toothed whales feed mainly on fish, squid, and octopus. Some whales also eat shrimp and other crustaceans. Killer whales sometimes catch seabirds and turtles!

SQUID

OCTOPUS

HERRING

A killer whale's mouth opens wide when it tries to catch its prey

FILTERING FOOD

Humpback whales catch their food using their baleen. Baleen, or whalebone, are the long, hair-lined plates inside a baleen whale's mouth. They help the whale to catch prey. As the whale swims forward, water filters through its open mouth. When the whale closes its mouth, the water is forced out, and tiny creatures are trapped inside the baleen.

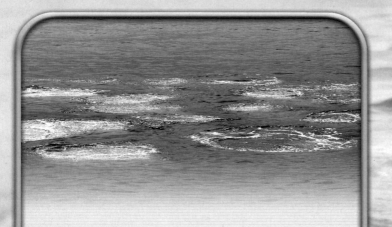

Bubble netting

A humpback whale swims up to the surface in a spiral, blowing air out of its blowhole. The bubbles rise up like a string of beads and trap krill inside a "net." The whale then surfaces and eats its meal. This is called bubble netting.

A humpback has up to 400 hairy baleen plates in its mouth

Trapping food

As a humpback gulps water and food, the grooves on its throat stretch so that it can catch more food. The water is squeezed out of its mouth through the baleen plates, but the food is trapped.

TALKING UNDERWATER

Dolphins use whistles, wails, clicks, and barks to talk to each other, to find their way, and to locate food. The clicking sounds that they make travel through the water and bounce off objects, sending back echoes. This is called echolocation, and dolphins use it to find food, but the sounds that they make are probably the loudest in the animal kingdom. Whale songs travel many miles underwater.

Lob tailing

Sometimes whales splash their tails on the surface of the water to show other whales where they are. This is called lob tailing.

Dolphin speak

Dolphins sometimes squawk at each other when they are quarreling. A dolphin can open its mouth without choking because it uses its blowhole for breathing and not its mouth.

Chatty whale

The beluga is nicknamed the "singing whale" and the "sea canary" because it makes so many different sounds. The beluga also makes faces, probably as a signal to others. Scientists are not sure what these expressions mean.

When a dolphin whistles loudly to its companions, bubbles may come out of the blowhole on its head

The beluga whale is the only whale that can change the shape of its lips.

When the mouth curls up, it looks as if the whale is smiling.

The fatty lump on the beluga's head can change shape too.

When the lump is big, the beluga is signaling to other whales.

21

DANCING DOLPHINS

Dusky dolphins are friendly and playful. They enjoy swimming alongside boats and leaping high into the air. These dolphins live in family groups, and several groups may join up to form a herd. Dusky dolphins feed on all kinds of prey, including squid and deep-sea fish.

Acrobats of the ocean

Dusky dolphins are probably the most acrobatic of all the dolphins. They can leap up to 17 feet (5 meters) into the air to do a somersault, then land on their backs with a big splash.

Herd of dusky dolphins racing a tourist boat

Happy families

The killer whale is also called an orca. These creatures live in every ocean, especially the cold Arctic and Antarctic oceans. Orcas live and hunt together in family groups called pods. There can be up to 55 animals in one pod. The chief male has a fin on its back that can be almost 6.5 feet (2 meters) tall!

Young killer whales stay close to their mothers for several years.

WATER BABIES

Whales and dolphins give birth underwater, and their young are able to swim right away. A baby dolphin or whale is called a calf. A bottlenose dolphin calf is about 3 feet (1 meter) long when it is born, and its fins are bendable. The calf feeds on its mother's milk for many months before it begins to catch its own food. The mother teaches and protects her calf for nearly two years.

Bottlenose dolphin
giving birth

1. While the baby dolphin is being born, another female, called an "aunt," helps the mother and protects her from sharks.

2. The baby dolphin is born in shallow water near the surface. Dolphins and whales are always born tail first.

An adult female helps protect a mother and baby

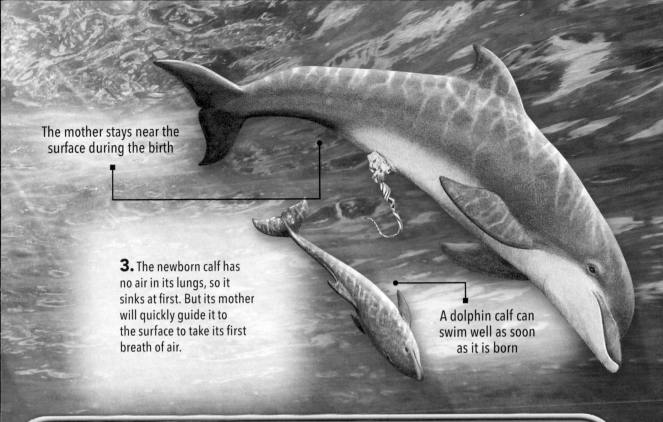

The mother stays near the surface during the birth

3. The newborn calf has no air in its lungs, so it sinks at first. But its mother will quickly guide it to the surface to take its first breath of air.

A dolphin calf can swim well as soon as it is born

Gray whale migration

Every year gray whales swim thousands of miles to breed and to feed. This is called migration. The gray whale's migration is up and down the western coast of North America. In the summer gray whales feed in the cold waters off the coast of Alaska. In the winter, females give birth in the warm water off the coast of California. A mother and baby swim together, close to the shore. At two months old a calf must swim 6,200 miles (10,000 kilometers) with its mother.

WHALES IN DANGER

For hundreds of years people hunted whales for their baleen, blubber, oil, and meat. Today whales and dolphins are still in danger. Many are trapped in fishing nets and drown. Others are killed by pollution when oil leaks from ships. Sometimes a herd becomes stranded on the shore and cannot get back to the sea. When this happens, people try to make the whales comfortable until the tide comes in again.

Stranded pilot whales

A whale cannot breathe on land because its heavy body squashes its lungs, so the animal must be returned to the water as quickly as possible. People can help by keeping whales wet with seawater so that their skin does not dry out. Water must never go inside the blowhole.

Trapped in a net

When people fish for tuna, they often catch dolphins by mistake. Dolphins become trapped in the nets when they chase the fish. In some countries people now catch tuna with a rod and line instead of a net. Tuna that is caught this way is called "dolphin-friendly" tuna.

Whales are rolled over gently so that they are lying right side up

Helpers protect pilot whales from the Sun with towels and seawater

DOLPHINS AND US

People have been fascinated by dolphins for thousands of years. There are stories of dolphins saving people from drowning and helping fishermen catch fish. Some of these tales are true! Dolphins are smart, playful creatures that enjoy swimming with humans. They often look as if they are smiling, which is possibly why we like them so much.

Meeting dolphins

Hector's dolphins are not at all shy, and they will approach beaches to play with swimmers, especially children! When people swim with dolphins, they should not touch them on the head.

All in a spin

Spinner dolphins are so named because they often leap out of the water and spin around and around. They can spin around as many as seven times before falling back into the water!

STUDYING WHALES

You can see whales and dolphins in every ocean of the world. In some countries people go whale watching on boats. By studying these majestic creatures in their natural home, scientists are able to learn how they feed and breed, and can help them to survive in the wild.

Tagging dolphins

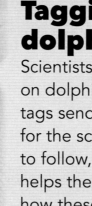

Scientists put tags on dolphins. The tags send out signals for the scientists to follow, which helps them discover how these animals behave in the wild.

Every humpback's tail looks different. Each tail has its own markings

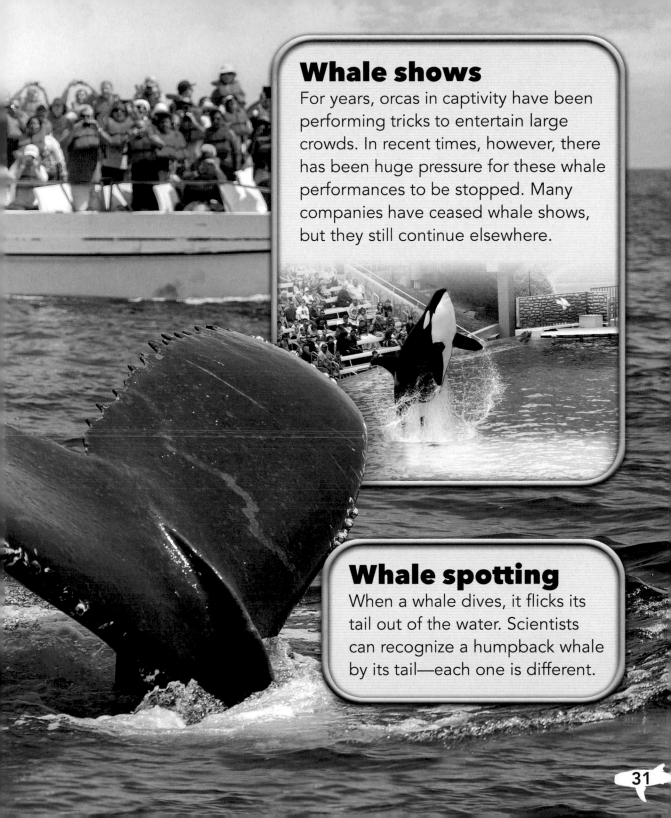

Whale shows

For years, orcas in captivity have been performing tricks to entertain large crowds. In recent times, however, there has been huge pressure for these whale performances to be stopped. Many companies have ceased whale shows, but they still continue elsewhere.

Whale spotting

When a whale dives, it flicks its tail out of the water. Scientists can recognize a humpback whale by its tail—each one is different.

GLOSSARY

baleen The long, hair-lined plates inside the mouths of baleen whales. Baleen works like a sieve to trap tiny sea creatures, and it can grow to over 13 feet (4 meters) long.

blubber The thick layer of fat beneath the skin of a whale or dolphin that keeps it warm.

breaching When a whale or dolphin rises up out of the water and falls back down with a big splash.

calf A baby whale, dolphin, cow, or elephant.

camouflage The coloring that helps a whale blend in with its surroundings.

captive A captive animal is one that does not live in the wild. Captive whales and dolphins usually live in aquariums.

carnivores Animals that kill and eat other animals.

crustaceans Animals such as crabs and shrimp.

echolocation How toothed whales find their way and find food. They send out sounds that bounce off objects and come back to them as echoes. These tell them how far away an object is.

evolve To develop gradually. Animals and plants have evolved over millions of years.

extinct When a type of animal no longer lives on Earth, it is extinct. *Basilosaurus* is extinct.

herd A large group of mammals that live together. Whales, dolphins, cattle, and elephants live in herds.

krill Shrimplike crustaceans that live in huge swarms in the southern oceans.

mammal A warm-blooded animal, such as a whale, that feeds its young on milk.

migration The movement of animals, such as whales, from one area to another. Whales migrate to find food.

plankton Tiny creatures and plants that live in the sea.

pod A group of related whales or dolphins.

porpoising The movement of dolphins as they leap out of the water in an arc.

predator An animal that hunts other animals. A killer whale is known as a predator because it hunts seals and dolphins.

prey Any creature that is killed and eaten by another animal.

stranding When whales or dolphins are stuck, or stranded, on a beach.

tusk An animal's tooth that grows very long. Male narwhals have one tusk.

whaling Hunting whales for their oil, blubber, and baleen—also known as whalebone.

INDEX